Every Now Is a Yes

poems by

Kathleen Wade

Finishing Line Press
Georgetown, Kentucky

Every Now Is a Yes

For Dorothy Stockelman Wade,
who made our house a home
our backyard a garden
our growing up a lesson in how to harmonize

For Debby

ACKNOWLEDGMENTS

The author acknowledges these journals and platforms for publication of
versions of poems appearing in this book:

Ohio Teachers Write, Ohio Council of Teachers of English Language
Illuminations: An Anthology of Teachers' Writing, Plymouth Writers Group
Love and Trouble: Anthology of Teachers' Writing, Plymouth Writers Group
For A Better World, SOS Art Cincinnati.com, Ghosn Publishing
Neighborhood Poets Laureate, Cincinnati Recreation Commission Publishers
Shelter in This Place: Meditations on 2020, Steiner House Books
Medium

Publisher: Leah Huete de Maines
Editor: Christen Kincaid
Cover Art: Forrest G. Brandt
Author Photo: Cecily L. Claytor
Cover Design: Kathleen Wade

Order online: www.finishinglinepress.com
also available on amazon.com

Author inquiries and mail orders:
Finishing Line Press
PO Box 1626
Georgetown, Kentucky 40324
USA

Table of Contents

Darkroom Directions...1

Street Poets...2

Wilson, Kansas..3

Feeding Our Finches..4

Stable Embrace...5

Clutch of Eggs..6

Beach Mothers..7

A Garden of Girls..8

Holding Her...9

Stepdaughter...10

My Mother's Place...11

Time..12

Delia..13

Me Too: 1971...14

City Stoop: 1967...15

Protest in the Laundry Room...16

White Privilege...17

Overlook at Mile 53...18

An Ordinary Guy...19

Crossings..20

Invisible..21

Leelah's Story...22

Their Dark Night...23

Panhandler..24

The Other Starry Night...25

Holy Ground..26

On the Thames..27

Really Long Distance...28

Saving a Sparrow..29

A Gift of Starlings...30

Clouds..31

Like the Sun...32

We Are the Light..33

Meditation at Shoreline..34

Darkroom Directions

Barely breathing, place the paper
glowing red and drop the easel.
Click. A milky image flashes.
Seconds pass. With dancing hand
dodge the beam or burn it deeper.
Click. Lift and submerge the sheet
in liquid thick with chemicals
and stir the silver out of hiding.
Elusive grays in patches and lines
seep from stark white. A skeleton
takes shape, sharpens dark
and bright with flesh and shadow.
Stroke and coax. Inspire.
And when you see that it is good,
slip and dip the sheet from tray
to dripping tray. An image
shimmers into being.

Tremble.

Street Poets

Swing, swing, my front porch calls. Summer sun
bakes our yellow brick house on Sinton where
we struggle restoring our neglected Victorian home.
I take a break from sanding floors, patching plaster,
step outside to my porch swing as babies cling
to their mothers parading outside to escape the heat,
smoking and waving at cars that throb with
pounding bass and rattling rap in angry rhymes.
So I swing while the girls shout at their kids
who cry and watch their cousins gliding by
on skateboards and bikes. Boys in hoodies and
baggy pants slouch at the corner, slap high-fives,
laugh out loud and balance boomboxes on their
skinny shoulders, playing *Hey you, baby,*
shake that thing. While I swing, swing, swing.

Wilson, Kansas

I was driving the 1950 Chevy heading west
to California from Ohio when you grabbed the wheel
and steered us off the Interstate onto an exit toward
a town not on the agenda I had so carefully drawn,
not knowing—since we were still newlyweds—how
nothing pleased you more than spur-of-the-moment.
There was only so much uprooting I could endure—
never having lived anywhere but my Midwest home—
while you coaxed me toward Berkeley.

Taking the plan, the mapping, the wheel away
was a final straw. The ancient car and the U-Haul trailer
slid to a shady curb in downtown Wilson, Kansas.
An argument about your tone of voice, the way
you never follow the plan spiraled out of control,
fueled by my fear of leaving everything, stoked
by your disappointment I couldn't go with the flow,
hurt that I couldn't hear your desire to share this
little surprise of a town with me. The ease and speed
with which you proposed a solution shocked.

You said I could take a Greyhound back to Ohio.
We'd split up our stuff, what I couldn't fit in luggage,
I could mail home, you'd take the stereo and albums,
your books and drive with the dog to Berkeley.
The mention of Sam slowed us down. We turned
to the back seat where our black lab sat watching,
his head between us, brown eyes steady, mouth poised
to drop his tongue to one side in the summer heat.

Here was the honest truth: Neither of us was willing
to give him up. We lifted the cooler lid, popped open
a Coors, made sandwiches, let Sam water the trees,
got back in the Chevy and continued moving West.

Feeding Our Finches

We stand side by side.
My hands soak in dishwater,
his wipe a wine glass dry.
We smile at the yellow glow of them,
their turn and twirl,
the flurry of their bodies on the feeder,
their song the music of colored glass beads.

Have we ever been happier,
this tall man standing next to me
at the sink, going grey,
fighting to keep his shape?
He is still the sandy-haired teacher
I chose decades ago,
careful historian, lover of music,
reader and writer, man of the world.

He cannot fix a leaky drain,
does not pick up his socks,
insists on a monthly cigar with the boys,
passes me over for football every Fall.

Still, most mornings he steps outside,
dips into a bin and scoops out feed
for the finches.
Pure gift, I am thinking,
this golden glow
we wear, side by side
at the kitchen window.

Stable Embrace

Each week I pass the stable
on my way to Pilates
leaving just enough time to pull over,
admire their majesty, muscle and shine,
long necks bending to munch pasture grass.

Today, just before Christmas, this:

Without the advantage of arms we humans
think we need to execute a kiss, without words,
the foreplay unfolding in black unblinking eyes
nostrils blaring heated billowy breath
condensing into the cloudy
snow-flecked air around them

without soft music save a cardinal's cheer
across the pasture frozen:

they bow and rub
blow and hiss
bobbing, nose-to-nose
their silhouette
tracing an inverted heart
against mid-morning,

they hold their embrace,
hold
posing

as if they've suddenly caught me
recording their love.

Clutch of Eggs

When the loggerhead female turns thirty, she crawls
from the ocean to do what female turtles
have done for three hundred fifty million years.

Each second year, this mother lumbers ashore,
carries her five hundred pounds to a sandy spot,
under a dark-green carapace wide as a yardstick.

On the darkest night in July she scans the tide,
inhales for predators, flings the sand on the beach,
releases and cradles the fertile eggs in her nest.

With her flippers she buries her steaming treasure,
then glides back to sea, her claws barely marking
the sand, her soft underbelly betraying no trail.

Should she sense danger, she'll dump her clutch
of eggs, all one hundred fifty, in the ocean,
rather than deliver them to an unsafe world.

Beach Mothers

I watch them reading their novels, shaded eyes
focused on their pages, their second sets of eyes
scanning the sand. And if the book should
capture them, another mother will leap
to snatch a child from certain peril.

I have seen mothers baking
beneath a layer of oil, deep in trance,
snap up like puppets and rush to stop a toddler
from toppling into a face full of sand
forever cleansing with mother spit.

In the midst of a half-dream
a mother will rise to settle fights, retrieve toy trucks,
crouch over tidepools in the sand, cradle
a diapered baby, shade the fair-haired.
When it's time to trod off to the steamy car,
she will cart it all on her hips and shoulders
absorbing the tantrums.

Knowing I'm past the age of motherhood,
I am tempted to sink in a nest of sadness,
until a baby toddles my way, smiling.
Sparkling in a silver spandex tutu
she stumbles toward my lone retreat,
her sandy hands and blonde curls blowing.
"Mama" she says, inviting me into the Clan.

A Garden of Girls

My girlhood dream persists
past menopause:
I'll be driving the Parkway
thinking, *Iris—she'd be first,
then Lily or Rose.
Next would come
Violet or Daisy—flower girls
I'd dress in colors
to match their names.*

I wonder sometimes
if my girls
found flesh and bone
in someone else.

Still, when I stand on the brink
of unbearable beauty,
as I do today on this stretch of sand,
the breaking waves and shells shattering
like glitter, I can almost feel
Iris, the first, twine her fingers
with mine. Or when the well
inside me is drained, a glint of light
will sparkle, as if she is gazing my way,
her azure eyes saying:

*I am here,
I am yours. You
birthed me years ago
along with Lily and Rose
and how many hundreds
of others named by other mothers.*

Holding Her

New from my niece's womb, she draws me
out of my hardened self. She is all soft curves.

Her head rolls freely. I am aware
of my stiffened neck no longer supple.

She fits in the bend of my arm, her fingers
are long and curl around mine. She knows

to connect, settles into the freedom
of being held. Her lips are round,

her tongue, tiny as a fingertip,
moves in and out. She is hungry.

Her eyelids flicker, she searches for light,
blinks at the sound of her mother's voice.

I love the warmth of her on my chest.
An untended hearth flares up in me.

Stepdaughter

Since I am slowly getting to know his daughter,
this overnight feels like a sacred trust. We lay out
sofa cushions for her four-year-old frame.
She thinks it's fine to sleep at the foot of our bed.

I lie awake, listen to her measured breathing,
occasional coughs, her kicking legs under her quilt.
My husband tosses and turns, finally decides
to move to the guest room to get a good night's sleep.

I doze off, dream I have stumbled onto a treasure,
something so precious I cannot do anything less
than carry it home, no matter the burden. I wake
to her moan of terror or pleasure—I cannot guess which.

She turns then settles. I prop myself up to watch.
Out of the darkness, I trace her body's outline—
her arm slung over her head in seeming abandon,
a tiny hand lies open across her forehead.

Eventually I fall back to sleep, but lightly.
I never return to my treasure-hunting dream.
This is the dream I dared not let myself have.

My Mother's Place

My mother was at home on her front porch, rocking.
The dinner dishes put away, the evening cooling,
she would sing and rock, letting her daughters climb
into her lap before bed. I can still feel the hum
of her voice, her soft stomach against my spine.

Damp and frayed from playing, I would beg her
to tell me stories about herself as a girl,
learning to harmonize on her mother's lap.
But watching her mother die was a story
my mother could not share.

How did she feel to be motherless at thirteen?
What was it like for her and her older sister
to tiptoe around their silent grieving father
and care for three younger girls—
no time for the comfort of rocking.

I picture a rocking chair on the front porch
where my mother grew up. Emma, her mother,
my grandmother, holds her baby girls,
she hums, whispers stories till the stars break open—
then the rocker is silent, her mother gone at forty.

My mother's place turned to steno school then a job
in a secretarial pool where she met my charming father
who sang and danced his way into her heart.
In a red-brick bungalow with a small front porch
she found her place singing in harmony, rocking.

Time

We didn't discover time, we invented it
to suit our obsessive-compulsive need
to control and judge and quantify everything.

I know this when I drive down Montfort Heights,
park my car and sit in front of the little brick bungalow
where I was born many decades ago. Yes, the driveway
wall is sagging, the wooden shutters are warped.

But wait: There sits my mother
in her favorite rocking chair on the porch,
crocheting lacy doilies, while apples simmer
into sauce on the kitchen stove, and white sheets
flap in the breeze on the backyard clothesline.

I am five, curled up on the studio couch
in our musty basement turning the gilded pages
of Mother Goose or exploring the garden in bud.
It is Spring again and daffodils have barely survived
an unseasonal snow. My father has cranked up
the Philco radio in Time for Opening Day.

Then a car passes by mine on the narrow street,
a stranger pulls back drapes at the front-room window
jolting me into the present—which is now—
which means it must be Time—though there's
no such thing—to turn the key and move on.

Delia

Who paid your way to America
after the famine scattered your brothers
to New York, St. Louis, Chicago?
Who hired you to cook and clean, 'til
you fell in love with the railroad man
who loved you but also loved his drink?

In homes you never owned, you birthed
two girls, my father, two more boys.
Take yourselves down to the train yard,
you'd say in your Irish brogue, *and pick up*
a bit o'coal that's dropped from the cars,
or there'll be no heat in this house a-tall.

In scrappy Lower Price Hill, you chased down
bullies with a stick, took in assorted cats,
dressed your girls in bows, made mutton stew,
and ruled the neighborhood in a street game
tossing a bean bag farther than anyone, ever.
You were my father's queen, singing him
Gaelic songs, passing on superstitions, laughing
at loss, protecting him from your husband's rage.

Before your oldest was twenty and your youngest ten,
you faded, leaving your children motherless.

I see your face fierce as a bulldog, your piercing eyes,
your short, athletic frame in my cousins, a sibling,
a few of my nieces. I have stood in the Galway cottage
where you and nine brothers and sisters were born,
smelled the peat bricks smoldering in the oven,
touched the dirt floor where you first stepped.

Tell me about your mother, I'd beg my father, and he
would fall into reverie, painting a picture of you
on Wilder Street, the sun against your back, undefeated.

Me Too: 1971

I am walking down Fourth Street, a few weeks into my first
real job after ten years as a nun. I am wearing a new red dress,
bought with my first real paycheck. I am feeling free, finally
a grown-up professional working woman, feeling lucky
I've landed a job at our local TV station, hoping I will
work my writing way into the production department,
even though I am starting at the switchboard.

It is lunch hour and I am noticing the way tall buildings
glow in the noonday sun, the way the shafts of light
scatter on the downtown sidewalk, when I hear his voice:
 "Hey Baby... you in the red dress..." The smooth brick walls
magnify the shouts from a loudspeaker four floors up.
I stiffen, measure my steps, feel my pounding heart,
the turn of my stomach with each new catcall.
 "Up here Sweetheart. Yeah, I like those legs...."

Without a thought, I stop, spot the grin beneath the yellow hard hat,
lift my lily-white former-nun's hand, poke my middle finger high
in the air in anger long-buried under a black religious habit.
Ripples of laughter, deep guffaws from the other guys
on construction crew echo off the walls: *"She got you, Bud!"*

I turn, keep on walking, enter the TV station, return to
my job, still shaking, knowing I will never forget the insult,
his smirk, his voice. In the ladies room I stare at my new red dress,
notice half-moons of underarm sweat, smile in approval
at my legs, and secretly arm myself for the future.

City Stoop: 1967

Delores planted herself on the front stone steps
most days around one. *Settin' a spell,* she'd say,
but that didn't mean she was ripe for talk.
I was a volunteer sent out to "meet 'n greet." I would
teach these lost souls to hope, get a job, go to school,
at the very least, I'd bring them into the fold.

Delores would smoke her Lucky Strikes, drink lemonade
from a jar and sit, eventually clearing a spot on the stoop
for me. Her *Yup and Nup* left no inroads. I gave up trying,
settled into a silence louder than her corner at 14th & Vine,
darker than her musty stairwell, heavier than the greasy summer air.

Sometimes Delores would sigh so deep it left her visibly lighter.
Her losses floated around us, dropped on my sandals,
fell into the folds of my skirt. Memories sat on our shoulders
and slid down our backs with the sweat from summer swelter.
Elbows propped on our knees, chins in the palms of our hands,
we'd sit. After a time, I'd pat her hand and move on.

Summer ended. I returned to my teaching where I felt the need
to dole out answers before the questions were asked.
One day I held up a glass of lemonade during lunch and
thought of Delores. I fell into longing for those scorching
afternoons on the city stoop where she taught me how to be quiet.

Protest in the Laundry Room

I am folding my husband's shirts,
smoothing the seams. I am
falling apart at the seams. I am
shaking the wrinkles from towels.
I am shaking inside. Can you tell?
Does it show? I wish I were forty
years younger and able to march.
I am longing to take a stand.
I stand instead in the laundry room
measuring liquid detergent,
pouring it into the tray while
a thousand young people holding
their flashlight phones in the air
in DC's Lafayette Square sing
"Lean on Me." I am leaning over
the sorting table letting my tears
fall on my husband's shirts. I sway
and lean with the young, in the
only way I can—the way I've done
everything—virtually—for months
since this deadly virus threatened us,
cautious of getting too close. I don't want
to distance myself. I want to shout,
to break things, to fall on my knee
for the man who is only the latest to die,
for all the named and unnamed others.
Instead I am folding the shirts.
I am folding in layers of sorrow
and sorting out rage. I am
leaning in with the chanting marchers.
I am folding and sorting,
singing my troubled heart,
soothing my weary soul.

White Privilege

It's up to me to loosen my grasp on my stockpile
of superiority, spread equity around, list the privileges
I take for granted: a seat on the bus, safety in a crowd,
a front-row ticket, a first-rate education, the absence of fear,
degrees, job offers and promotions, a secure future,
equity, deeds, titles, public pools, drinking fountains.

I want to see for myself the lynching museum, visit
the Antebellum South, but steer away from flowered
plantation parlors. I need to take a knee at the doors of
low-slung cabins — if any still exist — where slaves
(beautiful, bright) were born, beaten, broken.

I must admit my parents' black-faced minstrelsy,
it is my inheritance to own. I must apologize and
vow to change my advantaged mindset
before I can ever hope to change my heart.

I vow to live believing we are all equal human creatures,
promising to march when I can, helping others
into the virtual voting booth. Beginning again today,
I will listen to hard truths, I will act as if I believe
all politics is local and begins with me.

I will stop saying: … *but for the grace of God*….
This is not about God.

Overlook at Mile 53

A blue car driving north on the Interstate pulled
to the side and slowed to a stop on an overpass spanning
the Little Miami River. It was early morning rush hour
and commuters sped by without noticing a woman
in a red coat leaving her car, lifting one foot then the other
over the guardrail, stepping to the edge, pausing
then leaping to her death in the shallow riverbed below.

As children sat down to lunch in the cafeteria, and the
elementary school forged ahead without their principal
as if all would be well, a sheriff's deputy tracked down
the blue car abandoned on the side of the highway, headlights
still burning. At the same time, the red coat flapping in the
river's current caught the attention of nature lovers hiking
as they picked up litter on the east bank under the bridge.

Who would admit to spreading rumors that this gentle educator
had been seeing a woman? Had they sent letters, putting her job
in jeopardy? The fear of losing everything led her to spread
her arms and leap two-hundred-forty feet, freeing another
from ridicule, chaining them both forever to scandal,
silencing one heart—shattering the other.

An Ordinary Guy

He crossed the median in a pickup, striking a bus
full of kids from First Assembly of God who had
spent the day at Kings Island Amusement Park.
The bus's gas tank exploded. Six children found
the only exit. Twenty-seven more died, along with
the driver of the bus. Another thirty-four suffered injuries.

Hitler. Mussolini. Stalin: Names that live in infamy.
So too the driver whose name most have forgotten.
This was his second DUI—blood alcohol
at twenty-four percent—a mistake that cost him
sixteen years in prison, reduced by six for good
behavior, a reduction he declined to accept.

His name still burns in the memory of the survivors.
Ordinary guy from rural Kentucky, dropout who
earned his GED in prison, who joined AA and NA,
he now lives a private life a few miles from the site
where layered limestone rises on either side
of the highway, and evergreens dazzle the hillsides.

I wonder: Does he ever drive this patch of the Interstate—
if he drives at all? Does he ever read the marker*
which mercifully—or not—omits his name?
Aside from the injuries suffered that fiery night,
what other internal damage does he carry?
What else is crashing inside him, even now?

* *A sign on I-75 south near Louisville marks the site of the third-worst bus crash in US history.*

Crossings

A toddler floats face down at ocean's edge,
families in rickety boats sink in a foreign ocean,
others stretch out begging arms at the shoreline.

Land-locked and not knowing how to swim
they still climb into lifeboats without preservers—
or worse, with life jackets sure to pull them under.

Hope for her unborn child cannot save
a pregnant woman overcome by toxic fumes.

Crossing is dangerous. Danger is relative.
Risk is the pilgrim's silent partner.

I watch footage: flimsy wooden floats, packed with thousands
of bodies standing for days without food or water.
I can't forget hands in the air reaching
for somewhere safe. Surely those images must be

the reason I had to pull over on the Interstate
and weep at the sight of a land turtle, spinning,
upside down near the edge of the highway,
crossing in search of a swamp on the other side.

Crossing—risking all to answer a primal call
for safety and the promise of new life—
isn't that what we're all doing?

Then weep for the floating toddler,
the desperate parents,
the pregnant mother,
my ancient brother tortoise,
spinning,
upside down,
at the edge.

Invisible

Joshua mops floors in a Vermont hospital where
he has fled to escape slaughter in his native Congo.
He cleans American floors, but in his own country,
his own hospital, as Chief Surgeon, he did not do this work.

If he hopes to practice medicine again
he must study by day and mop floors by night.

To overcome despair he talks to his God
who answers, saying, *You will get through this.*
You are where you must be. You are of value.

He remembers the woman who mopped the floors
of his hospital in the Congo. He wants her to know
he finally understands how it feels to be invisible.

Leelah's Story

The ugly duckling (so the story goes)
suffers exile until she discovers
she's actually a swan.

I'm thinking of Josh,
a seventeen-year-old boy
who renames herself Leelah—
her parents' ugly transgender duckling.
She wants to be seen as a person
with valid feelings and human rights.

Unlike the duckling, she cannot
wait for the world to change.
One Sunday morning in December
she walks four miles
from her home to an Interstate,
into the path of a tractor-trailer.

Leelah had posted a message:
My death needs to mean something.

The ugly duckling in the fairy tale
lives happily ever after
with her family of swans.

But Leelah's story
is not a fairy tale,
and we are not swans.

Their Dark Night

Mystics have written of the dark night of the soul,
how the God they thought they loved abandoned them,
how prayerful glow turned dusky, leading through tunnels
of loneliness until lovelight burned through an opening
at the other end like a pinprick, body and soul emerging whole.
Transformation, mystics call it.

But who understands the dark night of the body—
the sure stark betrayal that same good God plays out
in them—in every mystic who knows but cannot translate,
knows even as the saints knew all is not as it seems?

Mirrors and measuring tapes chronicled betrayal of their body
which was theirs and not theirs—worked its hold on them—
beginning with dolls and dresses thrown aside as if they
were laced with poison, casting off names and games,
labels that toppled them into alien spaces and attractions
dark as night, traps they tried but could not escape.

Call the darkness what it is: denial, disowning, despair
dissolving at last in a shimmering light of understanding.
These trans-mystics give thanks in part to those who
held more than their hands: doctors in clinical coats
promising healing, a safe identity. Those who named them
but now call them another name. Those who wept and waited.

Trans-formational mystics survive by owning the darkness,
hoping to expose a body whose light they're gradually becoming
willing and able to see. Instead of daylight they take
the shadowy shades of acceptance, enough light and
love to keep them moving toward total transformation.

Panhandler

At a downtown stoplight,
snow and the temperature falling
two days before Christmas Eve
a man in an Army jacket,
wool cap, stubby beard, held up a sign:
Homeless. Anything Helps.
Next to him in the slush a backpack
sat on the curb. He was leaning
against a pole, staring at nothing.

Inside my head the debate raged on:
Will he spend it on booze?
Why isn't he in a shelter?
How does a handout solve anything?
You've asked the questions yourself.

The smallest bill I had was a five. I rolled
down my window, reached out to hand him
the money. As if he were just waking up,
he came to attention, then with careful steps,
approached my car. We were eye-to-eye.

The barriers that made us both
prisoners of our circumstances melted.

He smiled and whispered *Merry Christmas,*
as if we'd been planning to meet.
Then his eyes dimmed as he took the money
and stepped back from the car, back to the
corner pole and the backpack. *God bless you,*
I saw him say. The light flashed green.
I headed East, his blessing ringing in my ears.

The Other Starry Night

Vincent studied the night sky for its beauty,
not as astronomers do who chart the constellations.
He pictured an afterlife in the night sky,
wrote to his brother Theo: *Hope is in the stars.*

Unlike his more-famous Starry Nights, drawn from
memory and Vincent's untamed imagination, he painted
"Starry Night Over the Rhone" *en plein air*, at dusk
standing on the riverbank, near the Yellow House in Arles.

Each starburst, a tiny pyrotechnic explosion, competes
with glimmering yellow streamers from gaslit buildings
along the bank. In the foreground, lovers, arm in arm,
glance up asking: *What do you see that's so special?*

A century before the Hubble telescope's galaxies
flashed across our screensavers, Vincent loaded
his canvases with swirls and dots and clumps of paint
to show us the stars. All but his brother laughed

and thought him mad. Museum lines stretching
around the block don't begin to make reparation.

Holy Ground

Rain and cloud and mist smothered the barrier island
in North Carolina days before Christmas on this
darkest solstice night. When it cleared,
we bundled up and crossed the boardwalk over dunes
of oat grass and scrub. The fierce wind whipped,
waves crashed white on the shore sparkling with shells
broken to bits in a light so bright you could read by it.

The next evening, the skies still clear, we repeated
the ritual, the full moon blinding white and huge,
hanging over an ocean tamed, gentle waves unraveling
like silver ribbon, sprinkling foam and rhinestones
on the sand. Orion's belt and sword aglow,
we stood arm in arm without a word.

Silent night, holy night, I almost chanted.
I had to remove my shoes, I was surely on holy ground,
had to feel the rise and fall, the cold shock of being born,
waves washing over my feet sinking in the freezing sand.

Who'd stood here in 1866, the last time this perigee moon
kissed its companion earth? Battered by Civil War,
black and red-skinned farmers, sharecroppers,
fishermen tired and thin—what were their prayers
and longings as they planted their feet in this wet land?
Did they sing *All is calm, all is bright?*

Who will stand here in a hundred years—if this island
isn't underwater—when the ageless moon will again
be closest to earth? May they too marvel at the moon,
proclaiming: *We have seen a great light.*

On the Thames

Each time I've come to London I've glanced with disdain
at the gaudy signs announcing cruises along the Thames
on colorful boats where witty crewmen tell tall tales.

Instead I've stood aloof on bridges, gazed at the inky river,
imagined the barges and tugboats chugging up and down
carrying kings and maidens, thugs and ruffians. I've pictured
merchants with bales and batches of fish and fowl,
nutmeg and saffron, China teas, navigating their trades.

Today I surrender, pay the fare, zip up my coat,
wrap my scarf around me, and lean toward the flow,
expecting reflections of the Tower, the bridges,
the circling London Eye to catch my eye. They do.

But I'm on the budget cruise which stops to pick up
and drop off (let's just say it) *tourists*, so by the time
we float down and back, completing the loop,
I've been tied to shore watching the river ripple by,
black to blue, green to brown then black again.

Too cold to reach out and touch, the river reaches for me.
Water is life, with dross and danger, I hear it say.
Lean close, ride it, before you drown or dry up.

At the boat's front window a child about six stands gazing,
eyes wide open, laughing to his mother, delight and wonder
in his face. *Look what you're missing,* the river whispers,
being a grown-up all filled up with yourself.

Really Long Distance

The story of Itaru Sasaki's "wind phone" and the 2011 Tsunami survivors, was first heard in "One Last Thing Before I Go" on NPR's "This American Life," September 23, 2016, Miki Meek producer.

Because he believed the line between living and dead
is thin, a man in the seaside town of Otsuchi, Japan,
built a booth with a rotary phone in his hilltop garden.
He lit incense, rang a bell, picked up the unconnected phone
and began a ritual of talking to his lost relatives.

Tsunami survivors learned of the magic wind phone.
Thousands flocked to his garden to call those swept away,
dialed the familiar numbers, and began speaking:
Hello Father? Why did you leave without goodbye?
Hello Mother. Will I see you again? I am so lonely.

Their faces betrayed the fear and grief they carried.
Once in the booth their tears turned to comfort.
They left the booth smiling, joyful amid their tears.
Accustomed to silent suffering, they found a direct line
to the afterlife, in a phone booth on a solitary hilltop.

Saving a Sparrow

"Sometimes things happen that are hard to understand."
—*Mister Rogers, on finding a dead bird in his yard*

My cat at the glass door is how I discover
the young sparrow, his leg caught in our
wrought iron deck chair. Beneath the bird,
a white patch of droppings shows how dehydrated
he's become after struggling most of the day.

To curb my fear of flying things, I pray to
Saint Francis, who loved all creatures,
grab a bath towel, then step outside, keeping
our curious cat indoors. The sparrow's wings
flap wildly, his twig of a leg is twisted, red, swollen.

I surround the panting bird with the towel
cup him in my hands, his wild heart beating.
His black-bead eyes stare back at me. I whisper
soothing words, unwind and straighten his leg,
say I am sorry he has slipped into such a trap,
say to myself he will not survive.

I carry him to a blooming honeysuckle thicket
where sparrows cluck and cheep—his family?
I ask the Saint where to release him, stoop
and set him down in the mulch.
He drags his leg a step, then flaps his wings,
disappearing into the honeysuckle perfume.

A Gift of Starlings

to look up from my desk at just
the right moment—to spot in the sky

a murmuration of starlings
crisscrossing the pale-blue palette

common, ancient birds dipping and twisting
wringing themselves like spotted chiffon

shape-shifting trickery to avoid
a predator bird pursuing, pecking

without ever penetrating their edge
ever-changing, expanding, contracting

separate yet one, disappearing from my
window frame, undulating eastward,

leaving an ancient vision of improvisation:
an unforgettable calling card.

Clouds

They hover or glide
in opposite directions
sliding past or over
their higher heavier sisters.
Once I studied the science
knew all their names:
cumulus, stratus, cirrus, nimbus.
But like the clouds, facts fade.

Today I only know
these contrary vapors
in their layered formations.
They preach to me:
Grab light when you can,
they say, *but don't ignore*
the lure
of beauty's
ever-changing
shadows.

Like the Sun

How can I tell everyone they are shining like the sun?
—Thomas Merton

Merton affirmed it when a vision
confirmed for him the truth
of our infusion in original Light.

Mornings I face East, repeating
his belief in that Light, but today
rain has thickened the veil.

I cannot see that sun—not even
the trails of distant streetlamps,
the flashing factory lights,

that tower with its blinking red eyes,
or the taillights of lumbering trucks
and cars snaking along the Interstate.

Still, I lift up Merton's words—

just as a flash of lightning pierces
the curtain of clouds—

just as the rain clatters to a roar—

just as a shroud of grey
blocks any shimmer of brightness—

just as the room I'm sitting in
grows dimmer—

even then
we shine.

We Are the Light

I keep returning
to this:

You and I
are the light
of the world
that same world-light
quantum physics tells us
is spiraling rainbow-colors
infusing everything.

Shall we believe it?

If you and I
are light
why am I
so afraid
to dance
with darkness?

Meditation at Shoreline

Everything I have ever done
has prepared me for this.
Everyone I have ever touched
has led me to this embrace.
Everywhere I have ever been
has brought me here.
Every now is a yes
unfolding.

Mockingbird's refrain,
slow moan of ocean breath,
swaying sea oats gleaming,
cricket's whistle,
our neighbor's flapping flag—
none of these could surprise
or delight if it were not
for all that went before.

Even this tiny seabird with its rusty song
would be only a bird among other birds
(greasy crows, squealing gulls, stalking sandpipers)
had it not been
for everything

everything

I have ever done.

With Thanks

To every teacher who has encouraged me, I owe thanks and my very life as a writer. Along with my family, I am also grateful to Mary Pierce Brosmer, founder of Women Writing for (a) Change, who invited me to teach at and eventually become the Executive Director of this writing community in Cincinnati, Ohio. To all those who have sat in writing circles with me, listening, thank you. Others include Dr. Tom Romano and Michael Ireland, who taught me the fine points of editing. So many other fellow poets have encouraged me: my husband, Forrest Brandt; writing partners Molly Kavanaugh, Jenny Stanton, Sally Schneider, Andrea Nichols, Sarah Hayward McCalla, Laurie Lambert, Diane Debevec, Christy Schmidt, Karen Jaquish; and especially Mary Ann Jansen and Jane Pugliano for their wisdom, generosity and deep listening.

Kathleen Wade began writing poetry around age eleven, after inheriting her father's hand-me-down Olympia typewriter. Her poems have appeared in a number of anthologies, including *The Plymouth Writers Group, Ohio Teachers Write, For a Better World, Inside Out:SOS Art Cincinnati, Shelter in This Place: Meditations on 2020, Medium.com*, and for several years in the City of Cincinnati's *Neighborhood Poets Laureate Anthology*. A non-fiction book, *Ordinary People, Extraordinary Lives*, was published in 2012. A fictional memoir, *Perfection*, was published in 2018.

Kathy is a fourth-generation Cincinnatian and has lived and worked in six distinct and interesting Cincinnati neighborhoods, except for one glorious year in Berkeley, California. She earned her B.A. from Xavier University and her M.Ed. from the University of Cincinnati. Following a career as an English and drama teacher, Kathy devoted a decade to facilitating writing classes and workshops at Women Writing for (a) Change, a writing community in Cincinnati. Most recently she has been the director of a leadership-development program for women religious and their associates. She lives with her husband in yet-another interesting Cincinnati neighborhood.

www.ingramcontent.com/pod-product-compliance
Lightning Source LLC
Chambersburg PA
CBHW020220090426
42734CB00008B/1146